Me and My Friends

I Can Take Turns

written by Daniel Nunn

illustrated by Clare Elsom

Chicago, Illinois

© 2015 Heinemann Library,
an imprint of Capstone Global Library, LLC
Chicago, Illinois

All rights reserved. No part of this publication may be reproduced or transmitted in any form or by any means, electronic or mechanical, including photocopying, recording, taping, or any information storage and retrieval system, without permission in writing from the publisher.

Edited by Brynn Baker
Designed by Steve Mead and Kyle Grenz
Production by Helen McCreath
Original illustrations © Clare Elsom
Originated by Capstone Global Library Ltd

Library of Congress Cataloging-in-Publication Data
Cataloging-in-publication information is on file with the Library of Congress.

ISBN 978-1-4846-0248-5 (paperback)
ISBN 978-1-4846-0258-4 (ebook PDF)

Contents

Taking Turns 4
Taking Turns Quiz 20
Picture Glossary 22
Index 22
Notes for Teachers
and Parents 23
In this Book 24

Taking Turns

We **take turns** on the slide.

Now it is my turn!

We take turns on the sled.

Now it is my turn!

We take turns on the piano.

Now it is my turn!

We take turns on the tablet.

Now it is my turn!

We take turns at the store.

Now it is my turn!

We take turns at the sink.

Now it is my turn!

We take turns with the **dice**.

Now it is my turn!

We take turns with the **jump rope**.

Now it is my turn!

Taking Turns Quiz

Which of these pictures shows taking turns?

Did taking turns make these children happy? Why? What happens if you don't take turns?

Picture Glossary

dice small cubes marked with one to six dots used to play games

jump rope a children's game in which a long rope is swung over and under the person jumping

take turns an opportunity to do something in rotation with other people

Index

dice 16
jump ropes 18
pianos 8
sinks 14
sleds 6
slides 4
stores 12
tablets 10

Notes for Teachers and Parents

BEFORE READING

Building Background: Ask children what it means to take turns. When do they take turns? What can happen if they don't take turns?

AFTER READING

Recall and reflection: Ask the class how children in the book took turns. (waiting to wash, sharing the tablet) What are some other activities you've had to take turns doing?

Sentence knowledge: Which punctuation mark is at the end of the sentence on page 5? (exclamation mark) How does the exclamation mark help us know how to read the sentence?

Word knowledge (phonics): Have children point to the word *sled* on page 6. Sound out the three phonemes in the word *sl/e/d*. Ask children to sound out each phoneme as they point to the letters, and then blend the sounds together to make the word *sled*. What words rhyme with *sled*? (bed, shed, head)

Word recognition: Have children count how many times the words *turn/turns* appear in the main text (not counting the quiz). (16)

AFTER-READING ACTIVITIES

Sing the following song to the tune "Frère Jacques" (or "Are You Sleeping").
First it's your turn. First it's your turn.
Then it's mine. Then it's mine.
We take turns and we share
That is fair. That is fair.

In this Book

Topic
taking turns

Topic Words and Phrases
dice
jump rope
my turn
piano
sink
sled
slide
store
tablet
take turns

Sentence stems
We ___ ___ on the __.
Then it is my ___ .
We ___ ___ with the ___ .
We___ ___ at the ___ .

High-frequency words
at
is
it
my
now
on
the
we
with